OPTICS

YESTERDAY'S SCIENCE
TODAY'S TECHNOLOGY
SCIENCE ACTIVITIES

OPTICS

ROBERT GARDNER

DRAWINGS BY DORIS ETTLINGER

TWENTY-FIRST CENTURY BOOKS

A DIVISION OF HENRY HOLT AND COMPANY / NEW YORK

Twenty-First Century Books
A Division of Henry Holt and Company, Inc.
115 West 18th Street
New York, NY 10011

Henry Holt® and colophon are trademarks of
Henry Holt and Company, Inc.
Publishers since 1866

Library of Congress Cataloging-in-Publication Data
Gardner, Robert, 1929–
Optics / Robert Gardner.—1st ed.
p.   cm.—(Yesterday's science, today's technology)
Includes index.
1. Optics—Juvenile literature.   [1. Optics—Experiments.
2. Light—Experiments.   3. Experiments.]
1. Title   II. Series: Gardner, Robert, 1929-
Yesterday's science, today's technology.
QC360.G38   1994
535—dc20   93-39833
                                                            CIP
                                                            AC
ISBN 0-8050-2852-8
First edition—1994

Printed in Mexico
All first editions are printed on acid-free paper ∞.

1   3   5   7   9   10   8   6   4   2

Photo Credits
p. 14: © Richard Megna/Fundamental Photographs, New York; p. 18: © Ken
Kay/Fundamental Photographs, New York; p. 23: © Richard Megna/Fundamental
Photographs, New York; p. 24: © Richard Megna/Fundamental Photographs, New York;
p. 33: © Eastman Kodak Company; p. 52: © Richard Megna/Fundamental Photographs,
New York; p. 53: compliments of Olympus America Inc.; p. 56: © Nikon Inc.; p. 64:
© Leonard Lessin/Peter Arnold, Inc.; p. 70: © Leonard Lessin/Peter Arnold, Inc.; p. 76:
© Orville Andrews/Photo Researchers, Inc.

CONTENTS

INTRODUCTION

Optics is the study of visible light and the devices (optical instruments) that make use of light. Optical instruments include cameras, eyeglasses, microscopes, telescopes, slide projectors, lasers, and so on. The development of useful optical instruments moved slowly before the seventeenth century. Even so, unlike the laws of gravity, which preceded space technology by 300 years, people devised and used optical technology before anyone attempted to explain the nature of light.

Plane (flat) mirrors date back to prehistory, and references to "burning glasses" (lenses) are found in early Greek writings. But the use of lenses to magnify was probably not developed before Arabians such as Alhazen (965–1039) investigated this property of lenses around 1000 A.D. It was 1609 before Galileo Galilei (1564–1642) turned the lenses in the telescope he had invented toward the moon and realized that his optical device could be used to bring the heavens closer to earth. Although Marcello Malpighi (1628–1694) is usually given credit for inventing the microscope in the 1650s, the technology required for such a device was in hand when Galileo developed his telescope.

It was nearly 1700 before Isaac Newton (1642–1727) and Christian Huygens (1629–1695) first developed comprehensive theories to explain the behavior of light. Their theories came well after the basic technology of lenses had been developed to a point where they could be used to make instruments as sophisticated as telescopes and microscopes.

In this book, you will investigate some of the scientific principles and technology involved in optics. Each chapter contains a number of activities designed to enhance your understanding of the subject. You will find a ✖ beside a few of the activities. The ✖ indicates that you should ask an adult to help you because the activity may involve an action or the use of something that might be dangerous. Be sure to find adult help before attempting activities marked in this way.

Some of the activities, which are preceded by a ★, might be appropriate starting points for a science fair project. Bear in mind, however, that judges at such contests are looking for original ideas and creative thinking. Projects copied from a book are not likely to impress anyone. However, you may find that one or more of the activities in this book will stimulate a project or experiment of your own design that will lead you to the winner's circle at your school's next science or invention fair.

1

THREE PROPERTIES
OF LIGHT

The simplest, though not the least expensive, optical instrument ever invented was the *camera obscura* shown in Figure 1. It was nothing more than a large lightproof room with a very tiny hole on one wall. The wall opposite the tiny hole was usually painted white to serve as a screen. Light coming through the hole would produce an image on a canvas as shown in the drawing. Some early artists used the camera obscura to provide a colored, upside-down image of a scene they wanted to paint. With the image on their easel, it became a matter of mixing paints to match nature's color. The rest was like using crayons and a coloring book.

As you see from the drawing, the formation of the image can be explained by assuming that light travels in straight lines. Shadows can be explained by using the same assumption; so, too, can the images seen in mirrors. But before you accept this assumption, you might like to build a small camera obscura of your own to see if such images really do form when light comes through a small opening.

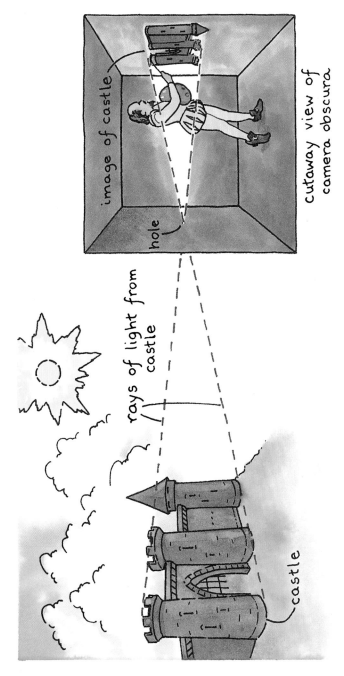

Figure 1. The camera obscura was used to make an image on a screen, wall, or canvas. Such an optical device allowed an artist to match nature's true colors.

A SMALL CAMERA OBSCURA

MATERIALS
- *T-pin*
- *shoebox*
- *scissors*
- *cardboard*
- *waxed paper*
- *tape*
- *light bulb and lamp*

To see how a camera obscura works, use a T-pin to make a pinhole in the center of one end of a shoebox. Use scissors to cut a small square hole about 1 cm (1/2 in.) on a side at the center of the other end of the box. Next, cut a piece of cardboard to divide the box in half as shown in Figure 2. Cut out a square about 5 cm (2 in.) on a side from the center of the cardboard. Tape a piece of waxed paper over the opening as shown. Finally, put the lid on the box.

Take the box into a dark room and turn on a single light bulb that you can view through the box (see Figure 3). Light from the bulb can enter the pinhole. If you look through the small peephole at the other end of the box, you can see the bulb's image on the waxed-paper screen. Is the bulb's image right side up or upside down? Can you expain why?

If the shoebox is a model of the camera obscura shown in Figure 1, what part of the box represents the wall opposite the pinhole? Where would a miniature artist stand to paint a picture of the light bulb?

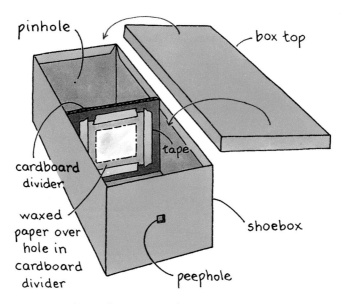

pinhole

box top

cardboard divider

tape

waxed paper over hole in cardboard divider

shoebox

peephole

Figure 2. A model of a camera obscura.

end of box with pinhole

waxed-paper screen inside box where image of bulb is formed

cardboard divider at middle of box (inside)

end of box with peephole

Figure 3. The bulb's image will appear on the waxed-paper screen at the middle of the box.

Move the cardboard divider with its waxed-paper screen until it is about one-quarter of the way from the pinhole to the hole you look through. Stand in the same place as before and repeat the experiment. What is different about the size of the image? Can you explain why?

Now move the divider until it is about three-quarters of the way from the pinhole to the hole you look through. Try to predict what effect this change will have on the size of the bulb's image on the screen. Then look at the image through the peephole. Was your prediction correct? If not, can you explain where you went wrong?

How does the size of the image change when you move the box closer to the bulb? Farther from the bulb? Can you explain why?

How do your experiments with a model camera obscura help to confirm the assumption that light travels in straight lines?

Reflected Light and Mirrors

Humans probably first saw their images when they gazed into the smooth surface of a pool, lake, or pond. But centuries before Christ, Egyptians had learned to make mirrors by polishing metals until they were very smooth. Some mirrors are still made that way today. By the sixteenth century, Venetian craftsmen were making mirrors by coating glass with a mixture of mercury and tin.

In 1835, Justus von Liebig (1803–1873) found that heating a mixture of formaldehyde, ammonia, and silver nitrate would deposit a fine layer of silver on glass supported above the mixture. This method, called silvering, is similar to the process used today to make most mirrors. More expensive mirrors are made by vaporizing aluminum in a vacuum chamber. The vapor condenses on a glass plate to form a very smooth, thin layer of metal.

We are so used to mirrors that we don't think of them as part of modern-day technology, but they are. Think of all the places you see them, on the sides of cars and trucks as well as in their headlights, in stores, hotel lobbies, and airports, on the walls of bedrooms and bathrooms. Where else can you find mirrors? What is the purpose of each mirror?

The surface of a mirror reflects a flashlight beam onto a card.

THE LAW OF REFLECTION

MATERIALS
- *dark room with light outside door*
- *sheet of white paper*
- *sheet of cardboard (depending on floor's surface)*
- *mirror*
- *pencil*
- *protractor*

At night, turn off all the lights in a room, such as your bedroom. Leave a bright light on outside the room. If you open the door just a crack, a very narrow beam of light will enter the room on each side of the door. Place a sheet of white paper on the floor so that the narrow light beam is visible on the paper (see Figure 4). If the room is carpeted, you'll need a sheet of cardboard beneath the paper. How does the light beam indicate that light travels in straight lines?

Place a mirror on the paper so that the light beam "bounces" (reflects) from the mirror. Hold the mirror steady while you use a pencil to carefully draw lines along the front surface of the mirror and along the middle of the path of the narrow beam before and after it hits the mirror.

Once you have made your drawing, use a protractor to measure the angle between the mirror and each ray—angles a and b in Figure 4. How do these two angles compare?

Repeat the experiment a number of times. In each trial, turn the mirror to change the angle between the beam and the mirror. How do angles a and b compare in each trial?

A consistent regularity about nature—one that can always

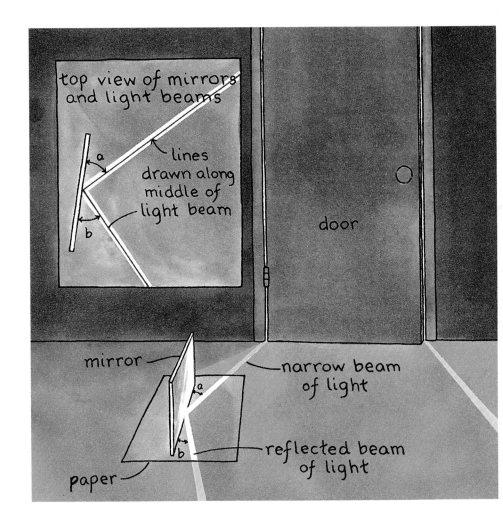

Figure 4. A mirror can be used to reflect a narrow beam of light coming through the crack in a door that is slightly ajar. How do angles a and b compare?

be observed and predicted—is called a law of nature. Here, for example, is a law of nature: Any object dropped near the earth's surface falls straight downward toward the center of the earth. In your experiments with the mirror, what regularity did you discover about angles a and b? How would you state this regularity as a law of nature?

LIGHT AND MIRRORS

MATERIALS

- *mirror*
- *piece of paper*
- *sheet of cardboard*
- *clay*
- *pencil*
- *T-pin or nail*
- *ruler*
- *protractor*
- *tall (long) pencil*

The photograph shows colored beams of light striking a horizontal mirror and being reflected. The protractor on the mirror enables us to measure the angles between the beams and an imaginary line perpendicular to the mirror because this line extends from the 0° line on the protractor to the point where the light is reflected. As you can see, the red beam that strikes the mirror makes an angle of 20° with this vertical line. The reflected red beam also makes an angle of 20° with the line. What is the angle between the green beam that strikes the mirror and the line perpendicular to the mirror? What is the angle between the reflected green beam and the vertical line? What about the blue beam and its reflection? Could you have predicted the angle for each reflected beam based on the experiment you did in Activity 2?

To see why images appear to form behind a mirror, place a mirror near the center of a piece of paper that rests on a sheet of cardboard. You can support the mirror with a small lump of clay as shown in Figure 5a. Use a pencil to draw a line along the rear surface of the mirror. (In most mirrors, reflection occurs on the rear surface where the mirror is silvered.) Now stick a T-pin or a nail that is about as tall as the mirror at a point approximately 10 cm (4 in.) in front of the mirror as shown. Remove the mirror, and use a ruler and pencil to draw two straight lines from the pin to the line that you drew along the back of the mirror. These two lines represent any two narrow beams of light (light rays) that might go from the pin to the mirror. There are, of course, millions of rays that you could draw, but two are sufficient for our purpose here.

From what you have learned about the way light reflects, use a protractor, ruler, and a pencil to draw the paths two light rays would follow after being reflected by the mirror. Then, using a ruler and pencil, extend your drawing of the reflected rays backwards beyond where the back of the mirror was located earlier. Extend the lines until they meet as shown in

Colored light beams show that the angle of incidence equals the angle of reflection.

Figure 5b. The point where the rays meet is the point from which they would appear to be coming if you saw them reflected from the mirror.

Put the mirror and pin (or nail) back in the same places they were before. This should be easy because you drew a line along the back edge of the mirror. What do you notice about the reflected rays you drew (r and r' in Figure 5b) and the images of i and i' in the mirror? What do you notice about the images of i and i' and the extensions of r an r' in the mirror?

Have a friend hold a tall pencil upright behind the mirror at the point where the two extended rays meet. Look in the mirror from behind the T-pin. Notice that the top of the pencil, which extends above the mirror, seems to be at the same place as the image of the T-pin that you see in the mirror. Notice, too, that the top of the pencil is in line with each of the two reflected rays you drew earlier. To see if the pencil really is at the position of the image, look again at the top of the pencil and the pin's image from behind the T-pin. Move your head slightly from side to side, or close first one eye and then the other. Does the top of the pencil above the mirror continue to "stick" close to the image of the pin? If it does, they must be at the same place.

To see that two things stick together in our vision when they are at the same place but not when they are at different places, try this experiment. Hold your right index finger upright at arm's length in front of your face. Place your left index finger about half an arm's length away. Now close first one eye and then the other. Notice how the images of your two fingers seem to shift when you change eyes. Next, place your left finger on top of your right one and again close first one eye and then the other. Notice that this time they stick together.

Do you think the pencil and the image of the pin will stick together if the pencil is held at a point in line with the pin's image but close to the back of the mirror? At a point well beyond the intersection of the lines? Try it! Were you right?

a.

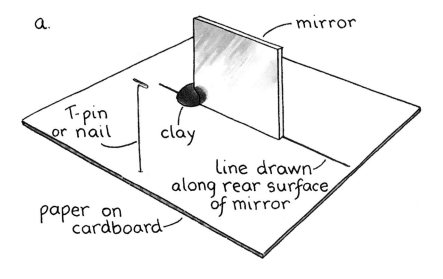

b.

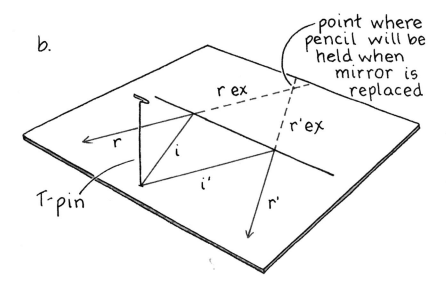

Figure 5: a. Experimental setup. b. Lines i and i' represent rays of light that go from the pin to the mirror. Lines r and r' represent the reflected rays of i and i'. Their direction can be predicted from the law of reflection. Lines r_{ex} and r'_{ex} are the extensions of r and r' behind the mirror.

Reflected Light and Refracted Light

You've seen that the angle at which light strikes a mirror is the same as the angle at which it is reflected. The next picture reveals another property of light. Notice that the paths of the blue, yellow, and red light beams coming in from the bottom of the picture are all bent as they pass from air into the glass prism. They are bent again as they emerge from the glass back into air. Whenever light passes from one transparent material to another, such as from air to glass or from glass to air, it is bent if it strikes at an angle other than 90° (other than perpendicular to the surface). We say the light is *refracted* (bent) as it passes from one substance to another. But, unlike reflected light, the angle between the light beam and the surface is not the same for the beam outside the glass as it is for the refracted beam inside the glass.

Look at the photograph carefully—you can see that not all of the light striking the glass is refracted; some of it is reflected. In fact, although you may not be able to see it, some light is reflected at both surfaces—as it enters and leaves the glass. Although glass, plastic, and other transparent substances transmit light, some light is reflected when it strikes their surfaces.

You've probably noticed that the blue light beam in the photograph is reflected once inside the prism. If you measure carefully, you'll find that the angles between the beams and the surface of the prism are the same before and after the light is reflected. It makes no difference whether light is reflected from a mirror or some other surface—the same law holds. The angle between the blue beam and the surface of the left side of the prism is so small, however, that all the light is reflected, none is refracted. This reflected blue light illustrates total internal reflection, a phenomenon you'll investigate more thoroughly in Chapter 2.

In the next photograph, you see three colored beams coming from the bottom of the picture. The model lens is tipped so as to intercept each beam at a different angle. The yellow beam shows very clearly that light is bent both as it enters and leaves the glass.

You may also notice that some yellow light is reflected at both surfaces of the lens when it enters and leaves the glass.

The blue beam strikes the glass at a greater angle (relative to a line perpendicular to the surface) and is refracted more (bent more) than the yellow light. Together, the yellow and blue beams show that the amount the light is refracted increases as the angle that the light strikes the lens increases. The blue beam is *not* refracted as it leaves the glass because it is perpendicular to the upper surface of the lens.

The red beam strikes the lower side of the lens at the smallest angle and is bent the least. However, the angle the refracted red beam makes with the upper surface of the lens is such that all the light is reflected back into the lens. In fact, the red light is reflected twice before it finally emerges along a vertical path from the upper surface of the lens—another illustration of total internal reflection.

Light's Properties and Optical Instruments

There is a law of nature that describes the relationships between the angle of incidence and the angle of refraction for all transparent materials, but it is not a simple one. You may study it later in a physics course. What is important here is the fact that light does bend (refract) when it passes from air to glass or vice versa. In fact, the reflection and refraction of light, as well as the straight-line paths that it follows in any one material, is all that's needed to understand most optical instruments.

In the next three chapters, you'll investigate a number of common optical instruments. By using the simple principles of reflection, refraction, and the straight-line paths followed by light, you can understand how most of these instruments work.

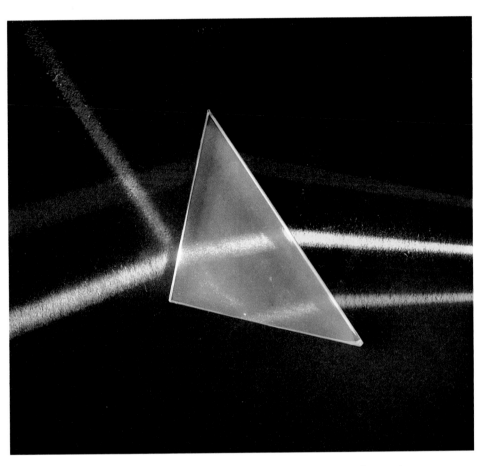

Light beams bend as they pass from air into a glass prism and bend again as they exit.

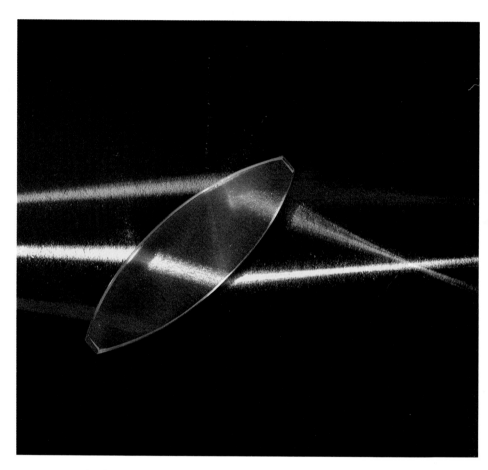

As the angle at which a light beam strikes a lens increases, so does the angle at which it is bent.

BUILD A PERISCOPE

MATERIALS
- *two or more mirrors*
- *cardboard or metal tubes, such as mailing tubes*
- *various tools, tape, glues, etc., depending on your design.*

As you know, periscopes can be used to see around corners. Others are used to see above the surface while a submarine remains hidden beneath the water. Where else are periscopes used?

Using what you know about reflection, design and construct your own periscope.

2

LENSES, LIGHT, AND MAGNIFIED IMAGES

Lenses were mentioned in the introduction as a way to make magnified images. A magnifying glass is the simplest use of a lens, but lenses are also used in slide, movie, and overhead projectors to produce large images on a screen. Combinations of lenses are used in microscopes and telescopes to bring, in a sense, the eye of the observer closer to the object being viewed.

In this chapter, you'll not only learn how a number of optical instruments work, but you'll also build working models of these instruments. You'll begin with a convex lens (one that's fatter in the middle than at its edge). Because of the convex surface, even parallel rays strike the lens at slightly different angles. The farther from the center of the lens, the greater the angle of incidence. The greater the angle of incidence, the more the light is refracted. Figure 6 shows parallel rays entering a convex lens. Notice that the farther the rays are from the center of the lens, the more they are bent. The point where the parallel rays come together (converge) is called the focal point of the lens. The distance between the lens and the focal point is called the focal length of the lens.

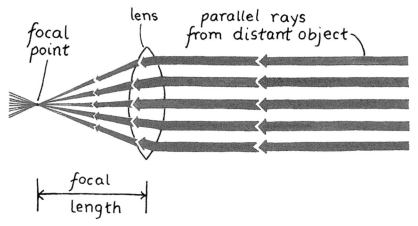

focal point

lens

parallel rays from distant object

focal length

Figure 6. A drawing showing the focal point and focal length of a convex lens.

★ **A C T I V I T Y   5**

A CONVEX LENS, ITS IMAGES,
AND ITS FOCAL LENGTH

MATERIALS
- *jar of water*
- *sunlight*
- *sheet of cardboard*
- *a convex lens*
- *a room with window and light-colored wall*
- *white card*
- *ruler*
- *study lamp with a frosted bulb*

A jar of water in sunlight will allow you to see how a convex surface converges (brings together) light by refraction. Hold the jar perpendicular to a bright beam of sunlight. Place a sheet of cardboard behind the jar. Notice how the sunlight is converged to form a bright line of light. If the container were curved in all directions—if it were a sphere instead of a cylinder—what would you have instead of a line of light?

To test your prediction, replace the jar of water with a convex lens. The surfaces of the lens have the curvature of a sphere. Move the lens back and forth in front of the cardboard so that the light striking the lens converges on the cardboard. Was your prediction correct?

Place a convex lens on the print on this page. Slowly raise the lens so it is farther from the print. What happens to the apparent size of the letters seen through the lens? What happens as you slowly move the lens even farther from the print?

To see the images formed when the lens is a long way from the objects being viewed, stand on the side of a room opposite a window. Look at the outdoor scene with the lens about half a meter (2 ft) in front of one eye. What do you notice about the images?

You can "capture" the images of these distant objects on a screen. Hold a white card behind the lens as shown in Figure 7a. The view through the window on the opposite side of the room can be seen on the screen in all its natural color. Images such as these are called real images. Unlike the images you see in a plane mirror (virtual images), which only appear to be behind the mirror, these images are real and can be seen on a screen.

The rays of light from a distant object that reach a lens are very nearly parallel. Therefore, the distance between the lens and the clear, small, sharp image of outdoors on the card is approximately the focal length of the lens. Use a ruler to find the approximate focal length of the lens you are using.

To convince yourself that the focal length you have measured is accurate, repeat the experiment using a very distant object such as the sun or moon. CAUTION: DO NOT LOOK AT THE SUN!

Not all real images are smaller than the objects that give

a.

convex lens

image

white card

b. convex lens

lamp

60W 120V

frosted bulb

120V
——
60W

image of print on wall

Figure 7: a. A real image of a scene can be captured on a screen by bringing light together with a convex lens. b. To see a real image larger than the object from which the light comes, hold the lens so it is slightly more than its focal length from the subject.

rise to them. Place a study lamp with a frosted bulb about a meter (yard) from a light-colored wall as shown in Figure 7b. Be sure the bulb is turned so the print on its surface can be read. Hold the lens near the bulb and move it slowly back and forth until you find on the wall a sharp image of the print on the bulb's surface. Are the images on the wall larger or smaller than the actual size of the letters and numbers? Has the print been turned upside down by the lens? Has it been reversed left for right?

Can you obtain a real image if you hold the lens so it is *less than* one focal length from the print on the bulb?

Find the approximate focal lengths of some other convex lenses. How is the focal length of a lens related to its convexity or roundness?

Convex Lenses and Two Kinds of Images

As you saw in Activity 5, a convex lens forms upright, enlarged images of an object when it is close to that object. When it is more than a focal length from the object, it forms inverted, real images, which may be larger or smaller than the object. Figure 8 shows how those images are formed. Notice that the images formed when the lens is less than a focal length from the object are similar to the virtual images formed by a plane mirror. They only appear to be behind the lens. The rays, which are diverging (spreading apart), appear to come from points on the image, which is behind the lens.

A hand lens, or magnifier, held near an object produces a virtual but enlarged image of the object. To form a real image, the object must be more than one focal length from the lens. Such an arrangement is used to produce images with a slide, overhead, or movie projector.

 ACTIVITY 6

LENSES AND PROJECTORS

MATERIALS
- *slide projector*
- *square piece of cardboard about 20 cm (8 in.) on a side*
- *scissors*
- *tape*
- *35-mm slide*
- *study lamp*
- *light-colored wall*
- *convex lens*
- *rough-surface screen such as a flattened egg carton*
- *white stick or ruler*
- *table lamp with a bright bulb*

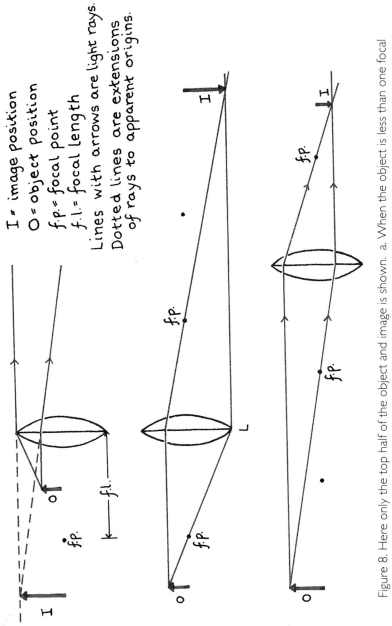

I = image position
O = object position
f.p. = focal point
f.l. = focal length
Lines with arrows are light rays.
Dotted lines are extensions
    of rays to apparent origins.

a.

b.

c.

Figure 8. Here only the top half of the object and image is shown. a. When the object is less than one focal length from the lens, the image is virtual and larger than the object. b. If the object is outside the focal length of the lens but close to it, the image is real and larger than the object. c. If the object is far from the lens (greater than two focal lengths), the image is real but smaller than the object.

- *dismantled cardboard box with sides longer than height of lamp and bulb*
- *mirror*

Examine a slide projector. You will find a bright light bulb and a concave reflector at one end. The reflector reflects light that would otherwise escape back through the bulb. This light then passes through a thick condensing lens, which absorbs heat and converges the light onto the slide. Most projectors also have a fan to help keep the slide cool. After passing through the slide, the light is refracted by a movable lens that is used to focus the slide's image on a screen.

To see how a slide projector works, cut a 4-cm (1.5-in.) square in a piece of cardboard about 20 cm (8 in.) on a side. Tape an old 35-mm slide over the opening in the cardboard. Hold the cardboard in front of a study lamp in an otherwise dark room. Let the light that comes through the slide fall on a light-colored wall about a meter (yard) from the lamp. Move a convex lens back and forth in front of the slide until you get

A slide projector uses a bright light bulb, a concave reflector, and a condensing lens.

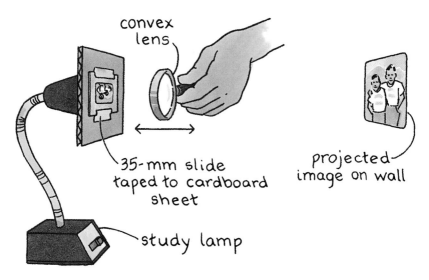

convex
lens

35-mm slide
taped to cardboard
sheet

projected
image on wall

study lamp

Figure 9. You can make a model of a slide projector like the one shown in this drawing. What parts of the projector are represented by each part of the model? What parts of the projector are not in the model?

a clear image on the wall (see Figure 9). How far is the lens from the slide when the image on the wall is clear?

Now move the lamp closer to the wall. From what you've done before, do you think the lens will have to be closer or farther from the slide than it was before to produce a clear image? Try it! Were you right? Try to predict where the lens will be when a clear image is found with the lamp several meters from the wall.

A movie projector is similar to a slide projector, but it is more complicated because it has to flash a new image on the screen about every thirtieth of a second. If the movie has sound, there must be a sound system as well as the optics. As long as the projector flashes a new image on the screen every 1/20th of a second or less, we don't notice that the picture has changed. This is because the images that form on the retinas of our eyes require about 1/10th of a second to fade away.

One way to see the persistence of vision is to use a slide pro-

jector to produce an image of a slide on a nearby rough surface such as the inside surface of a flattened egg carton. The image will be very difficult to see. But if someone moves a white stick or ruler rapidly up and down just in front of the rough screen, the image will become quite visible. Can you explain why?

Your school probably has an overhead projector that you can examine. A model of such a projector can be made (see Figure 10). To avoid the danger of a fire, ask an adult to help you. In a dark room, a lamp with a bright bulb is placed about a meter (yard) from a light-colored wall and surrounded on three sides by a dismantled cardboard box. Place the sheet of cardboard that you used earlier in this activity above the bulb, resting on the top of the box. The cardboard should be several centimeters (at least 1 in.) above the bulb; the bulb should not touch the cardboard.

The opening in the cardboard represents the illuminated

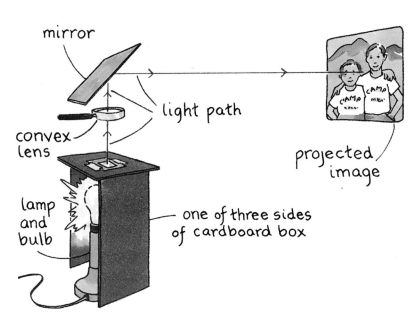

Figure 10. You can make a model of an overhead projector like the one shown in this drawing. What parts of the projector are represented by each part of the model?

35

platform of an overhead projector. The slide you used earlier in this activity can be used to represent a transparency. Hold a convex lens and a mirror above the slide. Move the lens up and down and adjust the angle of the mirror until you see a clearly projected image on the wall.

Lenses and Eyes

In addition to the lenses inside our eyes, many of us wear lenses (eyeglasses) in front of our eyes to correct visual defects. People with farsightedness (hyperopia) see distant objects more clearly than objects that are close. These people often have eyeballs that are shorter than normal (see Figure 11a). As a result, the light rays from

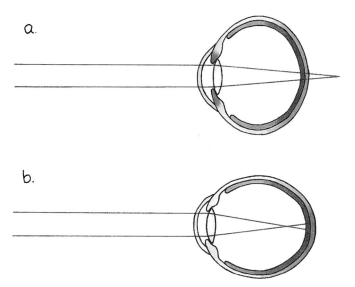

Figure 11: a. Farsightedness (hyperopia) is often the result of an eyeball that is shorter than normal. As a result, images of near objects are brought to focus behind the retina. b. Nearsightedness (myopia) can be the result of eyeballs that are longer than normal. Images of distant objects are focused in front of the retina.

near objects are not refracted enough to converge on the retina. Instead, their point of focus lies behind the retina. The lens cannot be made fat enough to bring the rays together on the retina.

The opposite effect is nearsightedness or myopia. Nearsighted people frequently have eyeballs that are longer than normal. Diverging rays of light from near objects can be focused on the retina, but the nearly parallel rays from distant objects are refracted too much. They converge in front of the retina as shown in Figure 11b.

Eyeglasses or contact lenses can be used to correct these errors in vision. Farsighted people can wear convex lenses to supplement their own lenses in refracting light rays enough to bring them together on the retina instead of behind it. Nearsighted people can wear concave lenses to spread (diverge) the rays enough so they converge on the retina instead of in front of it. The corrective effects of these lenses are shown in Figure 12.

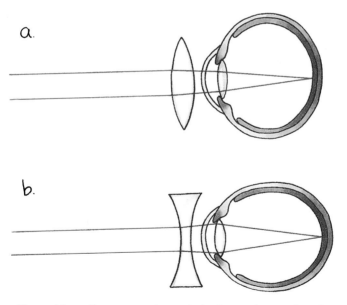

Figure 12: a. Convex eyeglasses help the eye's own lens to converge light rays so they meet on the retina. b. Concave eyeglasses diverge light so that the rays come together on the retina, not in front of it.

As you can see from Figure 12b, a concave lens spreads light rays apart—the opposite effect of a convex lens. Do you think a concave lens can produce real images? Virtual images? Would the images of objects formed by such lenses be larger or smaller than the objects themselves? Find a concave lens and use it to test your predictions.

Multiple Lenses: Microscopes, Telescopes, and Binoculars

Early microscopes consisted of a single fat lens that had a very short focal length. Such lenses can provide good magnification. But to provide even greater magnification and bring more of the unseen into view, early scientists began to build compound microscopes— microscopes with two lenses. In the case of telescopes, two lenses are necessary for magnification.

In the next two activities, you'll have an opportunity to build a telescope and a two-lens microscope. Expensive lenses are needed to make high-quality microscopes and telescopes, but building these instruments with simple lenses will help you understand the basic principles involved.

★ ACTIVITY 7

A TELESCOPE

MATERIALS

- *at least two convex lenses, one with a focal length of 20 to 30 cm (8 to 12 in.) or more, another with a shorter focal length— approximately 5 cm (2 in.) is good*
- *clay*
- *tape*
- *meter stick or yardstick*
- *white card*

A telescope can be made from two convex lenses. The lens closest to the object being viewed is the objective lens. It should have a focal length of 20 to 30 cm (8 to 12 in.) or more and should be a wide lens to capture as much light as possible. The second lens, closest to the observer, is the eyepiece. It should have a shorter focal length because the magnification depends on the ratio of the focal lengths of the two lenses. A lens with a focal length of approximately 5 cm (2 in.) will work well.

You can hold the lenses in your hands or use small chunks of clay on a meter stick or yardstick as shown in Figure 13a. Turn the objective lens toward some distant object. Use a white card to locate the real image formed by the lens and the lens's approximate focal length as you've done before. Place the eyepiece slightly beyond the focal point of the objective lens. The eyepiece lens will magnify the real image formed by the objective as seen in Figure 13b. Slowly

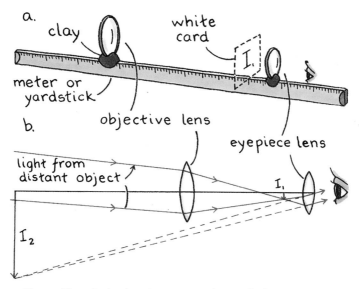

Figure 13: a. A simple telescope can be made from two convex lenses. b. Light is refracted by the objective lens to form a real image, I_1. The eyepiece magnifies the real image to form a virtual image, I_2.

move the eyepiece back and forth until you have maximum magnification.

Estimate the magnification of your telescope by opening both eyes and comparing the width or height of some part of the image with the same dimension of the actual object.

If possible, try several different lenses for objectives and eyepieces. Which combination gives the greatest magnification?

Reflecting telescopes are often used in astronomy. Such a telescope contains a concave mirror that produces real images (see Figure 14). A shaving or makeup mirror has a concave surface. If you hold it close to your face, you will see that it produces magnified images. But it will form real images of objects that are beyond its focal length. To see such images, take the mirror into a dimly lighted room and stand near a wall opposite a window. Turn the mirror toward the outdoor scene visible through the mirror. Move a white card back and forth in front of the mirror until you "capture" a real image of the scene on the card. What do you notice about the images?

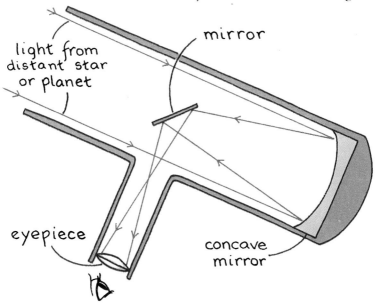

Figure 14. In an astronomical telescope, a small mirror reflects the light rays to an eyepiece.

A TWO-LENS MICROSCOPE

MATERIALS

- *mirror*
- *lamp or bright window*
- *microscope slide or clear piece of plastic*
- *sheet of cardboard*
- *scissors*
- *marking pen*
- *convex lens with focal length of approximately 5 cm (2 in.) or less*
- *convex lens with focal length of approximately 5 to 10 cm (2 to 4 in.)*
- *blocks and tape or other supports*
- *ruler*
- *small white card*

A microscope, like a telescope, can be made with two convex lenses. A mirror to reflect light through the specimen and into the lenses will be helpful. Support the mirror so that it reflects light from a bulb or bright window up through a small clear microscope slide or clear piece of plastic that is supported by a sheet of cardboard that has a hole in it (see Figure 15a).

Use a marking pen to make a very small "R" at the center of the clear slide or plastic plate. The tiny letter will serve as the specimen to be examined by your microscope. Hold the lens with a focal length of 5 cm (2 in.) or less over the letter. This will be the objective lens of the microscope. Raise the lens until it is slightly more than a focal length above the "specimen" so that the lens can form a magnified real image of the letter. To check, look down through the lens. You should see an inverted and enlarged image of the specimen.

Support the lens at this position with blocks and tape or with some other arrangement. To confirm the presence of an enlarged real image, move a small white card up and down above the lens. You should be able to find the exact position of the real image formed by the objective lens.

To obtain an even larger image, place the lens with a somewhat longer focal length above the first lens. This second lens will be the eyepiece of your microscope. It should be at a point a little *less than* its focal length above the real image created by the objective lens. In this way, it will act as a magnifying glass and produce an enlarged virtual image of the real image as shown in Figure 15b.

Adjust the position of your lenses slightly to obtain the greatest magnification of the letter. The letter and both lenses should lie along the same straight line. Make an estimate of the magnifying power of your microcope by holding a ruler near the image you see. Estimate the length of the magnified letter. Compare it with the length of the actual letter on the slide. What is the approximate magnifying power of your microscope?

If possible, examine a real microscope. It may have objective lenses with focal lengths measured in millimeters or less. How does the construction of the microscope ensure that the lenses will be directly in line with one another? What is the magnifying power of the microscope?

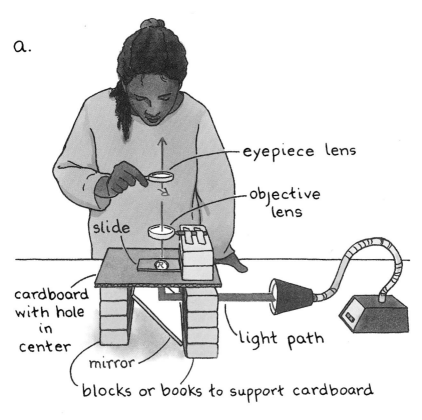

a.

eyepiece lens

objective lens

slide

cardboard with hole in center

light path

mirror

blocks or books to support cardboard

b.

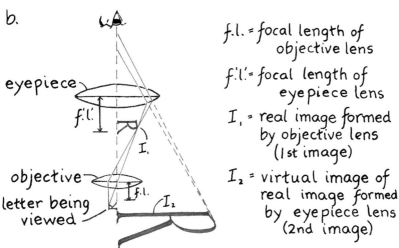

eyepiece

f.l.'

I₁

objective

letter being viewed

f.l.

I₂

f.l. = focal length of objective lens

f.l.' = focal length of eyepiece lens

I₁ = real image formed by objective lens (1st image)

I₂ = virtual image of real image formed by eyepiece lens (2nd image)

Figure 15: a. Building a two-lens microscope. b. The diagram shows how light rays are refracted to form a real, enlarged image, I₁, which is then magnified by the eyepiece to form an even larger virtual image, I₂.

Binoculars: Double Telescopes
With a Double Twist

As you've seen, a telescope produces an upside-down image that is also reversed right for left. Terrestrial telescopes—those used for viewing things on earth rather than stars or planets—often have a third convex lens to turn the image right side up. Binoculars, which are really two small parallel telescopes, one for each eye, often use prisms to make the images appear right side up. Figure 16 shows how the prisms and two lenses give rise to an image that has the same orientation as the object. Activity 9 will help you to understand how prisms can invert and reverse images right for left.

★ **ACTIVITY 9**

A PRISM, BINOCULARS,
AND TOTAL INTERNAL REFLECTION

MATERIALS
- *45-45-90 prism*
- *paper and pencil*
- *dark room with light outside door*
- *sunlight*

Draw the letter R on a small piece of paper. Place a 45-45-90 prism on the letter as shown in Figure 17a. Look into the largest flat surface of the prism—the one along the triangular prism's hypotenuse. You will see the regular R on the right and a reversed (left for right) R on the left. If you now turn the prism 90°, you can see a regular R with an inverted R above it (see Figure 17b).

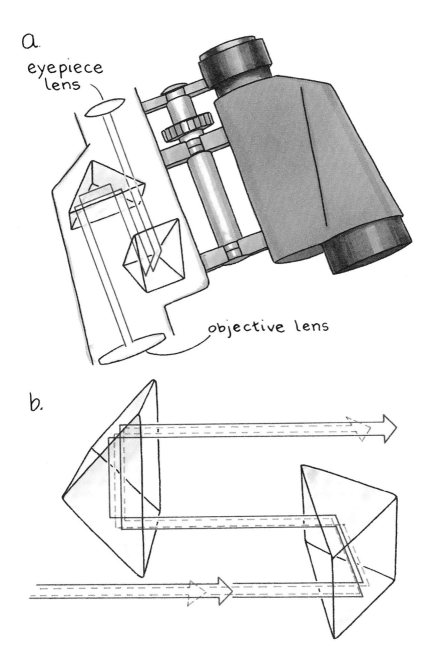

a.

eyepiece lens

objective lens

b.

Figure 16: a. Binoculars may use a pair of prisms to invert and reverse (right for left) the real image produced by the objective lens. b. A 3-D view of two prisms. Prism 1 reverses the image right for left. Prism 2 inverts the image.

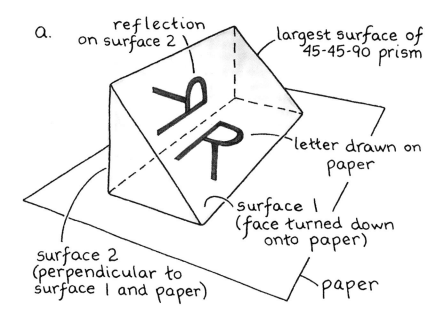

a. reflection on surface 2

largest surface of 45-45-90 prism

letter drawn on paper

surface 1 (face turned down onto paper)

surface 2 (perpendicular to surface 1 and paper)

paper

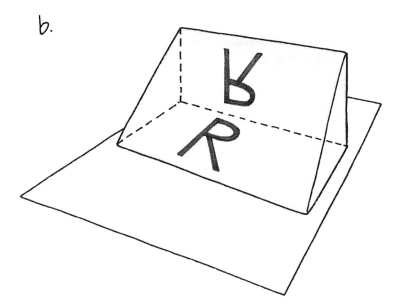

b.

Figure 17. Light passing through one surface of a prism is reflected by the surface perpendicular to the first surface. a. The R is reversed left for right upon reflection. b. The R is inverted upon reflection.

Using what you have learned in this activity, how do the prisms in binoculars invert and reverse the image produced by the objective lens?

If you have two prisms, arrange them so they produce an image like the one you would see using binoculars.

The use of prisms in binoculars can be made to illustrate another property of light, one that has been widely used in medicine. Slightly open a door as you did earlier to produce a narrow beam of light (see Activity 2). Place a sheet of paper on the light beam so it is easily seen. (If the room is carpeted, put cardboard under the paper.) Place the prism on the beam so that the light beam is perpendicular to the long side of the prism as shown in Figure 18a. This will cause the beam to strike one of the short sides inside the prism at an angle of 45°. Notice that none of the light in this beam goes through the short side of the prism. All of it is reflected to the other short side and back out the long face of the prism. As a result, the path of the light is turned 180°. It leaves the prism in the direction opposite to the way it came in. This failure of light to be refracted into air when it strikes a glass-air surface from within the glass at 45° is called *total internal reflection*. In fact, any light ray striking such a surface at any angle within the shaded area of Figure 18b will be reflected inside the glass. None will be refracted through that surface.

While you have the prism on the paper, turn it slightly as shown in Figure 18c to make the angle a little less than the so-called critical angle, which produces total internal reflection. Part of the light will emerge as a refracted beam. This beam almost touches the outside surface of the prism. Notice that the refracted beam is colored. In fact, it contains all the colors in the rainbow.

Look at the beam very closely. If necessary, examine the beam with a magnifier. Which color of light is refracted the most? The least?

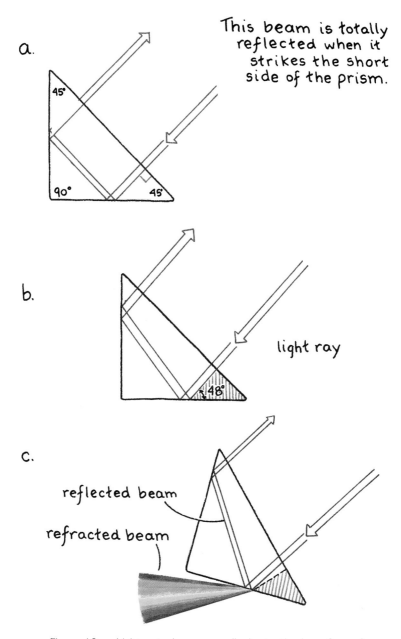

a.

This beam is totally reflected when it strikes the short side of the prism.

45°

90°   45°

b.

light ray

48°

c.

reflected beam

refracted beam

Figure 18: a. Light entering perpendicular to the long face of this 45-45-90 prism is totally reflected. None of the light is refracted through the shorter sides of the prism. b. Any light within the 48° shaded area is totally reflected. c. If the angle is changed slightly, a refracted beam emerges. It is separated into all the colors of the rainbow.

Brighter light, such as sunlight, will produce more intense colors. If possible, take a prism outdoors. Hold the prism in a beam of sunlight and turn it in front of a white surface until you see a rainbow of color. Do Not Look Directly at the Sun! It Can Damage Your Eyes!

A LIGHT GUIDE

MATERIALS

- *optical fiber light guide or optical fibers and black plastic tape*
- *large clear jar with screw-on lid*
- *water*
- *nail and hammer*
- *tape*
- *dark paper*
- *sink*
- *dark room*
- *bright flashlight*
- *board or block*
- *mirror*

You can buy an optical fiber light guide in a hobby store or from a scientific supply house, or you might borrow one from your school. Alternatively, you can make your own light guide by wrapping a foot-long bundle of several dozen optical fibers with black plastic tape.

To see how your light guide uses total internal reflection to transmit light, look into one end of the guide while you cover the other end with your finger. Now remove your finger and hold that end close to a window or another source of light. Can you see that light is transmitted along the optical fibers?

Bend the light guide into various shapes. Does light still follow the fibers when the guide is bent into various shapes?

Even water can be used as a light guide. Light moving from water into air will also be totally reflected at sufficiently large angles. However, for light moving from water to air, the shaded area in Figure 18b extends only to 41°. To see this effect, find a large jar that has a screw-on cover. Nearly fill the jar with water. Before you put the cover on the jar, use a nail and hammer to punch two holes in it. The hole that will be near the bottom of the jar when it is laid on its side should be about 1/2 cm (1/4 in.) in diameter. Water will flow out this hole. The upper hole can be smaller; it is simply a vent that will allow air to enter the jar as water flows out the bottom hole.

Cover both holes with tape and wrap the sides of the jar with dark paper. Lay the jar on its side with its lid over a sink as shown in Figure 19. Place a bright flashlight against the center of the bottom of the jar. You may need a board or block to support the flashlight at the correct height. Darken the room before you remove both pieces of tape so that water flows from the jar into the sink. Hold a mirror in the upper end of the stream where it is clear and smooth and has not yet broken into droplets. If you look into the mirror, you can see that light follows the stream of water. The light is brightest at the point where the water strikes the mirror.

Total Internal Reflection: A Useful Property

Light passing from air to glass will never be totally reflected. Even at angles close to 90°, some of the light will be refracted into the glass. But for light traveling from glass into air, it is totally reflected—no light emerges from the glass—at angles of incidence greater than 42° (as measured from a perpendicular to the surface). If the angle is measured between the beam and the surface, total internal reflection occurs when the angle is less than 48° (90°–42°).

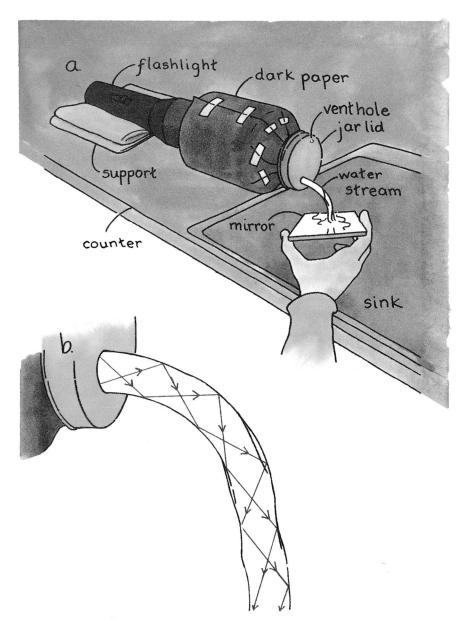

Figure 19: a. Apparatus to show that water can be used as a light guide. b. The arrows show the path of light rays in the water stream due to total internal reflection.

The red beam inside the lens in the photograph on page 18 was to-tally reflected twice inside the glass lens.

The next photograph shows a beam of blue light coming from the top of the picture and striking the long side of a 45-45-90 prism perpendicular to its surface. Since the beam is perpendicular to the long side (hypotenuse) of the prism, it is not refracted as it enters the glass and must, therefore, strike one of the short sides of the prism at an angle of 45°. Because an angle of 45° lies within the 48° shaded area of Figure 18b, the beam is totally reflected and none of the light is refracted. Why is the light totally reflected again when it strikes the other short side of the prism?

After the beam is reflected a second time inside the prism, it passes through the long side of the prism and reenters the air. Why

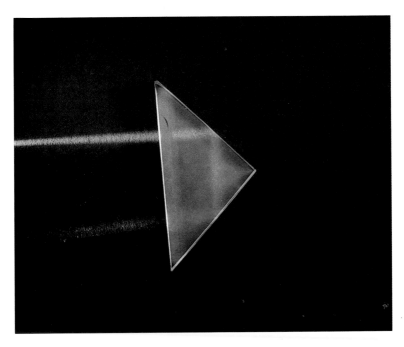

A light beam entering a prism perpendicular to its long side is totally reflected off both short sides.

An endoscope uses fiber optics as a light guide to let doctors view internal organs.

is the light not refracted as it moves from the glass prism into the air? What has happened to the direction the light beam is traveling after entering and leaving the prism?

By means of a light guide of flexible optical fibers and lenses, light can be carried inside the human body. A similar tube of fibers can carry reflected light back out. In this way a doctor can view organs and tissues inside a patient's body. The same tube that carries light can also carry air, water, and surgical instruments. By using these optical instruments, surgeons can perform operations without having to make incisions or by making only a small incision. Orthopedic surgeons now remove or repair knee cartilage after making a small incision just large enough to allow a flexible tube carrying optical fibers and special surgical tools to be inserted into the joint.

How are light guides used for nonmedical purposes?

3

CAMERAS AND PHOTOGRAPHY

We can often see in our mind's eye memorable events that have occurred in our lives, but those visions are fleeting and incomplete. The invention of the camera allowed us to capture and preserve on film the images formed in our eyes and brains. With a movie camera or a camcorder, we are able to preserve not merely images but entire events.

The Eye and the Camera

Although the technology that led to the camera was not based on the human eye, their similarity is remarkable, as you can see from Figure 20. Light enters the eye through the pupil—an opening in the iris, which is the colored portion of the eye. It enters the camera through an aperture in the diaphragm when a shutter is opened. The shutter corresponds to the human eyelid, which can prevent light from reaching the pupil. The size of the pupil or aperture can be increased in dim light to allow more light to enter. In both, a lens is used to converge light rays, onto the retina in the eye or the film in the camera, where an image forms as chemical changes take place. To record these images in dim light, more sensitive film is used in a camera. In the eye, images form on the color-sensitive

A typical camera operates in a way similar to the way a human eye works.

cells located at the center of the retina (the fovea) in bright light. In dim light, the more sensitive rod cells outside the fovea respond to the light, forming a less well-defined black and white image. The eye is lined with a black choroid coat that prevents light from being reflected inside the eye. A flat black surface inside the camera serves the same purpose.

Of course, there are differences between eye and camera. In the camera, light is focused by moving the lens, which usually consists of lens pieces rather than a single lens, farther from the film for near objects or closer for distant objects. In the eye, the shape of the lens changes. The lens fattens (becomes more convex) to focus light from near objects and becomes thinner when distant objects are viewed. Eye muscles control tension in the suspensory ligament, which, in turn, controls the shape of the lens. In addition, much of the refraction of light by the eye occurs in the cornea, while the lens is the sole light refractor in the camera.

A MODEL AND
A LOOK AT CAMERAS

MATERIALS
- *model of camera obscura built in Activity 1*
- *pencil*
- *convex lens*
- *white card—10 cm x 15 cm (4 in. x 6 in.)*

You can make a simple model of a camera from the camera obscura model you built in Activity 1. Enlarge the pinhole by pushing a pencil through it. Remove the waxed-paper screen and place a white card inside the box in front of the peephole. Turn the "camera" toward a scene viewed through a window. Move a lens back and forth inside the box to focus the scene on the white card.

In this model, what does the hole in the front of the box represent? What does the white card represent? What camera parts are missing in your model?

In the age of throwaway cameras, it doesn't make much sense to build your own. However, you will find it worthwhile to examine a number of cameras (without film) to compare their internal structures and compare their various engineering features.

A SLR (single lens reflex) camera has a mirror in front of the film (see Figure 20b). This allows the operator to use the same lens to view a subject and to converge light on the film. Normally the mirror, which lies between the film and the lens, is tilted at a 45° angle to reflect light up to the viewer. But when the shutter opens, a hingelike device flips the mirror upward so light can reach the film.

a. EYE

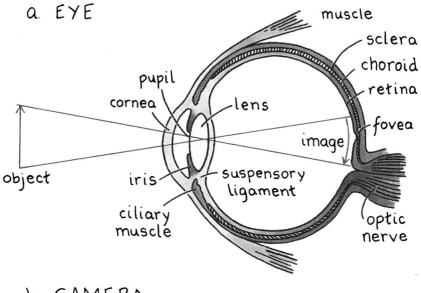

muscle
sclera
choroid
retina
pupil
cornea
lens
fovea
image
object
iris
suspensory ligament
ciliary muscle
optic nerve

b. CAMERA

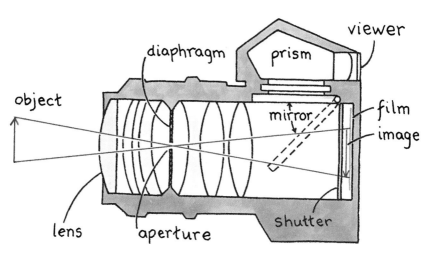

diaphragm
prism
viewer
object
mirror
film
image
lens
aperture
shutter

Figure 20. The eye, a, and the camera, b, are similar optical "instruments." But how are they different?

Black and White Photographs

The image formed by a lens is focused on the photographic film at the back of the camera. The film consists of a thin transparent plastic coated with an emulsion of gelatin that contains crystals of silver salts. Inside each crystal are tiny specks of pure silver, called sensitivity specks. When light strikes a crystal in the emulsion, electrons are released and collect around the sensitivity speck. Silver ions (positively charged silver atoms) in the crystals are attracted to the electrons and combine with them to form clumps of neutral silver atoms. These atoms gather in areas of the image where the light is intense. In areas that receive less light, fewer silver atoms are found.

The film is developed in a darkroom using a chemical solution. The solution increases the concentration of silver in those portions of the film that were exposed to light. The film is then washed in hypo (a solution of sodium thiosulfate), which dissolves and carries away the unexposed silver salts. What remains is called a negative. Because finely divided silver is black, the negative is dark where the light in the image was intense and clear where the image was dark.

The lens of an enlarger is used to produce a magnified image of the negative on photosensitive paper. The resulting photograph, or positive, will be light where the negative was dark and dark where the negative was light. The paper is then developed and fixed (washed) with hypo. The process is summarized by the drawings in Figure 21.

1.

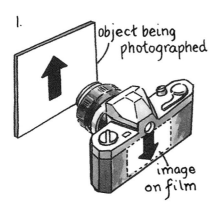 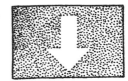

object being photographed

image on film

A photograph is taken with a camera.

Crystals exposed to light break down into silver.

2.

The film is developed. Fine dark particles of silver form where light struck the film. Unexposed crystals are dissolved by the developer. The resulting negative is washed (fixed) to remove silver salts.

3.

4.

An enlarger throws an image of the negative on photosensitive paper. Silver forms where light strikes the paper.

The paper is developed and fixed to provide a positive print.

Figure 21. The process of taking and developing a photograph.

ACTIVITY 12

MAKING PHOTOGRAMS

MATERIALS
- *studio proof paper (available at a photography store)*
- *sheet of cardboard*
- *objects such as a key, scissors, beads, a flower*
- *sunlight or bright light*
- *hypo (obtain from a photography store)*
- *tray*
- *cold running water*
- *spring-type clothespins*
- *newspapers*
- *heavy book*

Studio proof paper, unlike most photosensitive paper, does not change immediately when exposed to light. Place a sheet of studio proof paper on a piece of cardboard. Put some objects such as a key, scissors, beads, a flower, or other interesting objects on the paper. Then move the whole thing outdoors into sunlight or place it under a bright light. You will see the uncovered paper slowly change from white to dark red as the chemicals in the paper respond to light. Carry the cardboard and everything on it into a dimly lighted area. There you can remove the objects from the paper and view the photogram you have made.

If you want to preserve your photogram, you can fix it with hypo. Mix the hypo solution as directed and pour it into a tray. Dip the proof paper with your photogram into the solution for about two minutes. Then wash it in cold running water for about 10 minutes. Use clothespins to hang it up to dry. When the paper is dry, place it between newspapers and flatten it by putting it under a heavy book for several days.

When you have finished, the hypo can be emptied into the sink and flushed away with lots of water.

Color Photography

Although film for colored photographs was available as early as 1907, developing the film was so difficult that colored film for mass use did not appear until the 1950s. To understand color photography, you need to first know something about color and colored light.

<hr/>

ACTIVITY 13

THE MATHEMATICS
OF COLOR—ADDITION

MATERIALS
- *phonograph record or a compact disc*
- *white light bulb and lamp*
- *3 lamps (study lamps with cone-shaped metal shades work well)*
- *blue, green, and red light bulbs*

You saw in Activity 9 that a prism can be used to separate white light into a spectrum (all the colors of the rainbow). Another way to do this is to use an old phonograph record or a compact disc. Hold the record or disc so that light from a bulb a few feet away is reflected to your eye at a large angle as shown in Figure 22. You'll see that the white light is separated into a spectrum.

Just as white light can be separated into its component colors, the colors that make up white light can be added together to make other colors including white. To add one colored light to another, shine the colored lights on a white screen or wall so that they overlap. This procedure can be done in a variety of ways. One method is to use blue, green, and red light bulbs that can be purchased in a supermarket. Put the bulbs in separate lamps and shine the lights on a white screen or wall.

As you can see, the addition of blue and red light produces a pinkish purple color called magenta. Blue and green light combine to make a bluish green color called cyan. What is the color of the light when red light is added to green light? When red, green, and blue lights are all combined?

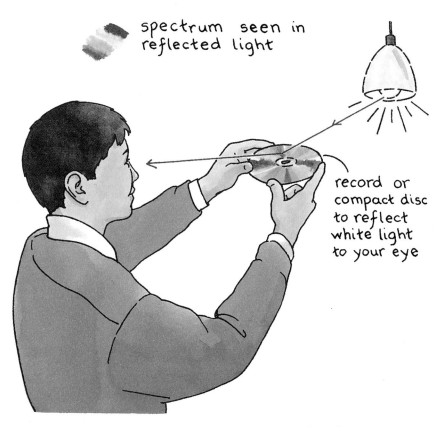

Figure 22. A phonograph record or compact disc can break reflected white light into a spectrum (all the colors of the rainbow).

63

The photograph shows what happens when beams of blue, green, and red lights overlap (are added together) on a screen. These three colors are called the additive primary colors of light because all other colors can be made by adding them together. As you can see from the picture, the sum of all three primaries is white light.

If you didn't succeed in making white light by mixing light from the red, green, and blue bulbs, try adjusting the intensities of the different colors by changing the distances of the bulbs from the wall or screen.

Color Photography: Part I

As you've seen, all the colors of light, including white, can be made by adding just three colored lights—blue, green, and red. That is why systems for making color photographs provide a means of combining those three colors. White light is first separated into the

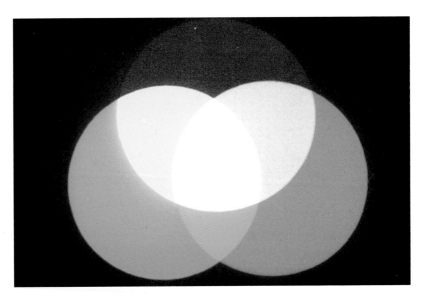

Blue, green, and red, the additive primaries of light, can be combined in various ways to make all other colors.

colors of which it is composed and then recombined to produce the colors that were present in the original scene viewed through the camera.

The colors are separated by the film, which consists of separate layers that respond to different colors in white light. Figure 23a shows a film with three color-sensitive layers. The layers are stacked with clear spacers in between. Figure 23b shows separate bands of light—black (no light), white, blue, green, and red—shining on the film. Silver is deposited in those layers that receive the colored light to which they are sensitive. For example, in the drawing silver is deposited in the top or blue-sensitive layer by the blue and white bands of light. Green light in the green and white bands causes silver to form in the middle layer, and red light in the red and the white bands leads to silver deposits in the bottom layer of film.

The silver salts in the film layers are coupled with dyes. During development of the film (Figure 23c), the dyes that couple with the silver in the film are yellow, magenta, and cyan. The dye in the blue-sensitive layer is yellow. Magenta pigments are produced in the layer that is green sensitive, and cyan dyes are formed in the red-sensitive layer. The black silver is then washed away leaving only the colored dyes.

Why is a yellow dye used to couple with silver in the blue-sensitive layer? Why is magenta used with the green-sensitive layer and cyan with the red-sensitive layer? Activity 14 will help you to answer these questions.

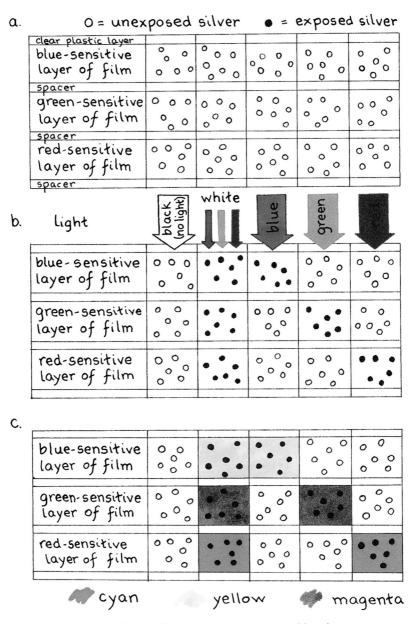

Figure 23: a. Color film has three color-sensitive layers. b. When color film is exposed, silver forms in those layers that receive colored light to which they are sensitive. c. During development of the film, dyes coupled with the silver appear. The silver is then washed away.

MATHEMATICS OF COLOR—
SUBTRACTION USING FILTERS

MATERIALS

- *colored sheets of cellophane, plastic, or gels used in theaters (red, green, blue, cyan, magenta, yellow)*
- *phonograph record or a compact disc*
- *white light bulb and lamp*

You'll need some colored sheets of cellophane, plastic, or even better, the gels used in theaters. (If you can't find such colored sheets, just read through this activity and go on to Activity 14b below.) Try to find sheets that are red, green, blue, cyan, magenta, and yellow. Once you have the sheets, look again at the spectrum reflected from the record or disc that you used in Activity 13. Ask a friend to hold one of the colored sheets in front of the light bulb as you look at the spectrum reflected from the record or disc. What parts (colors) of the spectrum come through each colored sheet? Which parts are absorbed?

A good red filter will absorb all colors other than those at the red end of the spectrum (red, orange, and some yellow). Similarly, a good blue filter will transmit only colored light in the blue region (violet and blue). A good green filter will allow only the central part of the spectrum (green and a little yellow and/or blue) to be transmitted.

Colored filters subtract some colors of light from a beam of white light. Using what you learned in Activity 13, can you predict what color or colors will be removed by a cyan filter? By a yellow filter? By a magenta filter? Have your friend hold each of these filters in front of a white light bulb while you look at the light reflected from a record or disc. Were your predictions correct?

Hold a magenta filter and a cyan filter back to back. Can you predict what colors will come through the combination? How about a magenta and a yellow filter? A cyan and a yellow filter? All three?

If your predictions are not right, it may be because the filters are not perfect. That is, a cyan filter may let through a little red light as well as blue and green. Check again the colors that pass through the filters using the white light and the record or disc.

MATHEMATICS OF COLOR—SUBTRACTION USING FOOD COLORING

MATERIALS
- *food coloring*
- *water*
- *clear, flat-bottomed plastic tumblers*
- *white paper*
- *strong light*

If you can't obtain colored filters, you can do something similar using food coloring, water, and clear, flat-bottomed plastic tumblers. Put a drop or two of blue, yellow, and red food coloring in separate tumblers. Add just enough water to each tumbler to obtain a transparent, richly colored liquid.

Often, blue food coloring reflects and transmits both blue and green light so it might better be labeled cyan. Similarly, red food coloring is likely to be magenta and reflect blue as well as red light.

What color do you see when you look down at a white

68

background through a combination of cyan and yellow solutions as shown in Figure 24? How can you explain what you see? Remember, cyan pigments transmit or reflect both green and blue light and absorb (subtract) red light. Yellow pigments transmit or reflect green and red light; they subtract blue light. What color is left when white light is transmitted through both cyan and yellow pigments?

What color do you see when you look down through both the cyan and the magenta solutions above a white background? Through both the magenta and cyan solutions? Through all three solutions? How can you explain your results?

The colors may not be exactly what you'd expect. Cyan food coloring may let through a little red light as well as blue and green. Similarly, yellow and magenta food colorings respectively may transmit some blue and green light.

Figure 24. What color do you see when you look through a combination of cyan and yellow solutions? Cyan and magenta? Magenta and yellow?

Figure 25 summarizes what you learned in Activity 14a or 14b. It shows how colored filters subtract colors from white light transmitted through the filter or how colored pigments subtract colors from the white light they reflect. The photograph shows the color of light transmitted through combinations of cyan, magenta, and yellow filters. These colors are called the subtractive primaries because a combination of all three of them will subtract all the color in white light.

Cyan and red are complementary colors because the combination of red and cyan light will produce white light. Remember, cyan is a combination of green and blue light. For the same reason, magenta and green are complementary colors. What would be the complementary color of blue light?

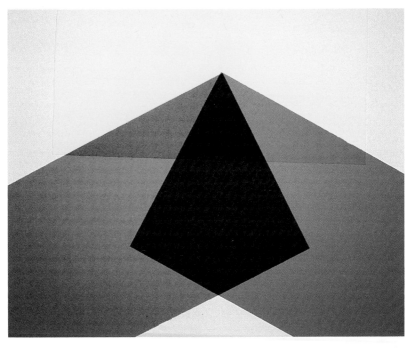

Cyan, magenta, and yellow, the subtractive primaries of light, can be combined to subtract all the color in white light.

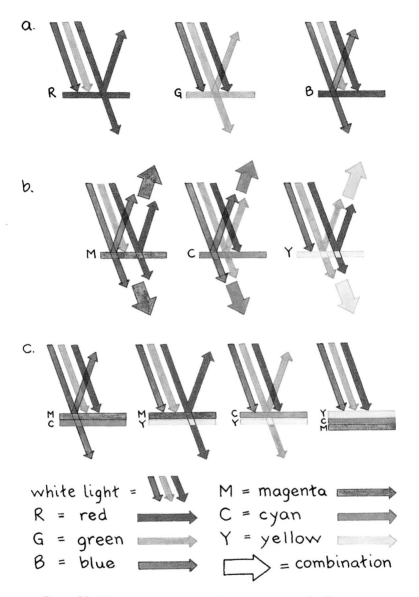

a.

R

G

B

b.

M

C

Y

c.

M
C

M
Y

C
Y

Y
C
M

white light =   M = magenta ⟹

R = red ⟹   C = cyan ⟹

G = green ⟹   Y = yellow ⟹

B = blue ⟹   ⟹ = combination

Figure 25. White light is shown striking a number of different colored filters or pigments in, say, cloth. Colored light that passes through the filters is shown emerging beneath them. Colored light reflected by the pigments in the cloth is shown being reflected above it. Various transmitted or reflected colors combine to form other colors.

A color photograph can be developed from the negative shown in Figure 23c. After the silver is washed away, white light is passed through the negative (Figure 26a) to form an image on the light-sensitive paper. As the drawing reveals, white light now comes through the band that originally received no light because no silver or dye was deposited there in any of the three layers of the negative.

The second band on the negative, which was illuminated by white light, transmits no light because dyes formed during development in all three layers. The three dyes—yellow, magenta, and cyan—combined subtract all the colors in white light. The next three bands of light coming through the negative are yellow (red + green), magenta (red + blue), and cyan (blue + green) as expected.

Figure 26b shows that these bands of light cause silver to be deposited in the layers of the photographic paper as they did those in the film. After developing the color print, the dyes formed in the paper (Figure 26c) will reflect the colors shown in the diagram. The first band will be dark because the yellow dye will absorb blue light, the magenta pigments will absorb green light, and the cyan dye will absorb red light, leaving very little light to be reflected. In the second band, there are no dyes, so all the light will be reflected. In the third band, there is no yellow dye to absorb blue light, so it will be reflected. In the fourth band, green light will be reflected because there is no magenta dye to absorb it. Cyan and yellow dyes will both reflect green light. Finally, the fifth band will be red—there is no cyan dye to absorb red light.

Figure 26: a. White light is shined on the negative developed from Figure 23c. b. The colors coming through the negative expose the photographic paper. c. The paper is developed to give the color print layers shown. The bands now reflect the same colors that are shown on the bands on the film in Figure 23b. Thus, the print has the same color pattern as the original "scene."

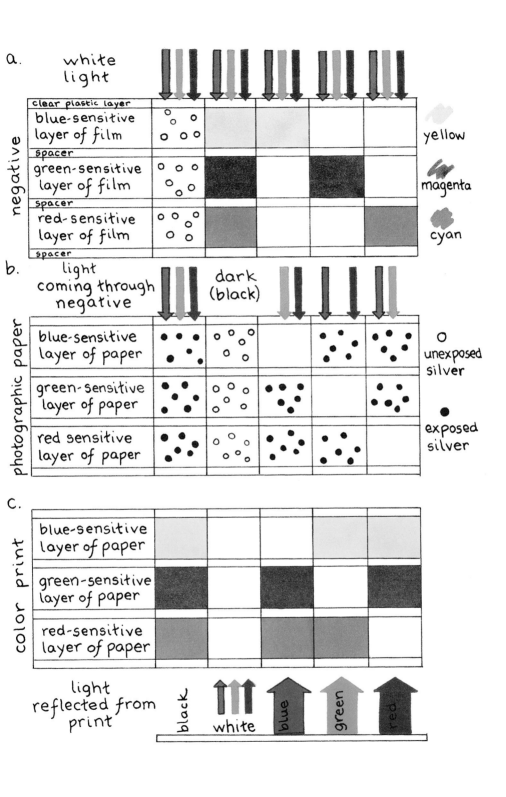

4

LASERS AND MORE

Another optical device that you've heard about and perhaps seen is the laser. Laser is an acronym for *L*ight *A*mplification by *S*timulated *E*mission of *R*adiation. The meaning of those words will become evident as you read on in this chapter.

A LASER'S BEAM

MATERIALS
- *low-power helium-neon laser*
- *chalkboard erasers*

Ask an adult to help you with this activity. Do Not Look Into a Laser Beam or Shine the Beam in Anyone's Eyes.

You may be able to borrow a low-power laser from your school or from someone who has a compact, battery-powered laser. Small, battery-powered lasers are commonly used as pointers at lectures or demonstrations.

Can you see the beam of red light from a laser beam when

you turn it on? Can you see the end of the beam if you point it at a wall or screen? Why can't you see the beam between the laser and the screen?

To make a laser beam visible, gently clap two chalkboard erasers together along the region where you expect to find the beam. Why does the beam become visible when you do this? You can also make the beam visible by holding a flat piece of cardboard near the front of the laser parallel to the beam.

How can you use a laser to demonstrate the reflection of a light beam? To demonstrate the refraction of a light beam?

Can the straight-line path of a laser beam be bent by a strong magnet? Design an experiment to find out.

An argon ion laser

A laser, as you've seen, produces an intense but very narrow beam of light. The beam remains very narrow over long distances because the light is coherent; that is, all the light waves have the same wavelength and "march" together, as shown in Figure 27a. Their crests (peaks) and troughs (valleys) are side by side.

As you probably know, matter is made up of atoms. Each atom has a tiny nucleus that contains a number of even tinier positively charged particles (protons). An equal number of negatively charged particles (electrons) move in orbits around the nucleus. The atoms of different elements have different numbers of electrons and protons. That's what makes iron atoms different from aluminum atoms or oxygen atoms. A hydrogen atom, for example, has one proton and one electron. A helium atom has two protons and two neutral particles (neutrons) in the nucleus, as well as two electrons in orbit, as shown in Figure 28a. Electrons are not limited to one orbit. By absorbing just the right amount of energy, an electron can "jump" to an orbit farther from the nucleus (Figure 28b).

Electrons that have "jumped" to bigger orbits eventually "fall" back to smaller orbits. When they "fall," they give off light. The light given off when an electron falls from one orbit to another

Figure 27: a. Laser light is coherent. All the light waves have the same wavelength and "march" together. b. Ordinary light is not coherent. The wavelengths may be the same, but they don't "march" together.

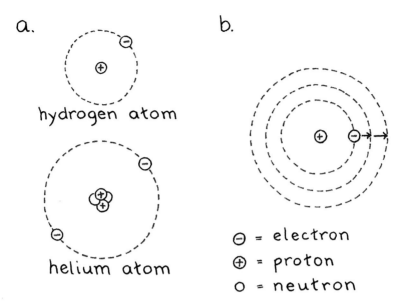

a.

b.

hydrogen atom

helium atom

⊖ = electron
⊕ = proton
○ = neutron

Figure 28: a. Each atom consists of a tiny nucleus, made up of positively charged protons, and an equal number of negatively charged electrons that are in orbits about the nucleus. b. By absorbing energy, an electron can "jump" to an orbit farther from the nucleus.

has a very specific wavelength and, therefore, a very definite color. If it falls to a different orbit, the wavelength and color of the light emitted will be different.

In a laser, there are atoms that absorb energy. An atom that has absorbed energy is said to be "excited." In an excited atom, an electron has moved to an orbit farther from the nucleus (Figure 29a). After a short time, the electron "falls" back to its original orbit, releasing light of a particular wavelength. The light released when an electron falls from orbit 3 to orbit 1 will have a different wavelength than that released when an electron falls from orbit 2 to orbit 1. However, all the light emitted by atoms of the same element whose electrons fall from orbit 2 to orbit 1 will have exactly the same wavelength.

Unlike other optical instruments you have studied, the laser was

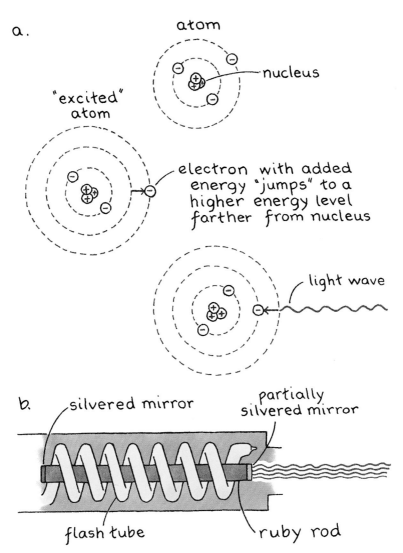

a.

atom

nucleus

"excited" atom

electron with added energy "jumps" to a higher energy level farther from nucleus

light wave

b.

silvered mirror

partially silvered mirror

flash tube

ruby rod

Figure 29: a. When an atom absorbs energy, an electron in the atom "jumps" to a larger orbit. When the electron "falls" back, it releases light of a particular wavelength. b. In a ruby laser, some atoms are excited by light from a flash tube. As the electrons in these excited atoms drop back to their original orbits, they release red light that stimulates other excited atoms to do the same. This red light is reflected back and forth along the ruby rod until (after a very short time) a beam of coherent light emerges through the partially silvered mirror at the front of the laser.

based on scientific theory. As early as 1917, Albert Einstein (1879–1955) had shown that according to theory it should be possible for an electron falling back to a smaller orbit in one excited atom to stimulate other excited atoms to do the same thing. His calculations also led him to believe that such stimulated changes would result in the emission of radiation (light) that was coherent. In 1954, Charles Townes and Arthur Schawlow at Columbia University produced a coherent beam of microwaves with a device called a maser (*M*icrowave *A*mplification by *S*timulated *E*mission of *R*adiation). In 1960, Theo Maiman discovered a way to produce a coherent beam of visible light using a ruby crystal. It was the world's first laser.

Figure 29b is a diagram of a ruby laser. Atoms in a ruby rod are excited by the green light from a flash tube that surrounds the rod. The electrons in these excited atoms quickly fall to an intermediate orbit and then, more slowly, to their original orbit. The drop from the intermediate to the original level is accompanied by the release of red light. When a wave of this red light passes by another excited atom, it stimulates that atom's electron to fall back to its original orbit and release its own red light. These two waves moving along the axis of the ruby rod can now stimulate two more excited atoms to release their light and move in the same direction. As this process continues, a large amount of red light is produced with waves that move coherently along the axis of the rod.

Some of the light escapes through the sides of the crystal, but the waves moving along the axis of the rod continue to stimulate light emission from additional atoms as they are reflected back and forth by the concave mirrors at the ends of the rod. The mirror at the back of the laser reflects all the light that strikes it, but the front mirror is only partially silvered. It may reflect 90 percent of the light, which stimulates more atoms to release more light. The rest of the light passes through the front mirror producing the laser beam.

All lasers work in similar ways; however, they may use different materials—crystals, liquids, even gases. When lasers were first invented, many people thought they were interesting but useless. They were soon proven wrong. The coherent beam makes it ideal for surveying or measuring large distances. By timing a laser pulse from earth to moon and back, the moon's distance can be measured to within centimeters.

Laser beams can be made so powerful and focused into such a small area that they can be used to weld metals. On the other hand, less powerful lasers can be used to repair a detached retina. Lasers are used in supermarket checkout counters to read the coded prices on items; they can read, too, the digital outputs of compact discs; and they are used to produce three-dimensional pictures called holograms.

Powerful lasers have been used to fuse tiny pellets of hydrogen into helium—a process that releases vast amounts of energy, a process that may replace fossil fuels as our major source of electric power. While a practical technology for fusing hydrogen and releasing its enormous energy in a controlled fashion has yet to be developed, lasers are likely to play a vital role in achieving this goal.

GOING FURTHER

In this book you have seen only a small portion of the science and technology of optics. There is much more that you can investigate. Some of the things you might like to investigate are listed below.

★ • If film is added to a camera obscura, it is called a pinhole camera. Design and build your own pinhole camera. You'll find the exposure times are on the order of minutes rather than seconds, so be patient. What kind of photographs can be taken with a pinhole camera? How is the quality of the image affected by the size of the pinhole? What happens if you make two pinholes?

★ • How can shadows be used to demonstrate that light travels in straight lines? To demonstrate that rays of sunlight are not perfectly parallel?

• Why are two lenses necessary to produce magnification with a telescope?

★ • How is the size of the aperture in a camera related to depth of field?

★ • What controls the amount of light that reaches the film in a camera?

Here are some photographic projects that you might enjoy. Perhaps you can find some of your own.

★ • Take trick photographs, such as someone appearing to hold small people in the palm of each hand. Such a photo can be taken by having one person kneel in a large field with hands out to his or her side, while two other people farther away stand so they appear to be on the first person's palms. This example is probably all you need to spark the design of a great many trick photographs of your own.

★ • Take photographs involving reflections. For example, if you photograph the images of trees or buildings reflected in the still water of a pond or lake, can people tell whether the photo is right side up or upside down?

★ • Long exposure photographs taken at night can produce some interesting results. For example, you might focus your camera on the North Star. By leaving the camera's shutter open for an hour or more, you can produce star trails—the paths of the stars near the apparently motionless North Star.

★ • Other photographic techniques or activities that you might find interesting include photographing fast-moving objects, aerial photography, photos taken through microscopes, telescopes, or binoculars, underwater photography, double exposures, and fun photos that provide unusual views of common objects or photos of unusual objects that can be used as "mystery" photos.

GLOSSARY

additive primary colors: blue, green, and red light. These three colors are called primary because all other colors can be made by adding these three together in various intensities.

cone cells: cells located in the retina of the eye. They are abundant near the center of the retina (the fovea) and are capable of detecting color.

critical angle: the angle at which all light is reflected within a transparent substance; no refracted light emerges.

cyan: the color formed by adding blue and green light together or by subtracting red light from white light.

electrons: negatively charged particles with very little mass. In atoms, the electrons make up the outer part of the atom that surrounds the nucleus.

focal length: the distance between a lens or curved mirror and the focal point.

focal point: the point where parallel light rays converge (come together).

hyperopia: farsightedness. People with hyperopia see distant objects more clearly than objects that are close by. They often have eyeballs that are shorter than normal so that light rays from near objects are not refracted enough to converge on the retina.

Laser: an acronym for *Light Amplification by Stimulated Emission of Radiation*. A laser produces coherent light as atoms, which are the source of the light, give up identical amounts of energy.

law of nature: a consistent regularity found in nature that can always be observed and predicted.

law of reflection: the angle between a light ray and the mirror from which it is reflected is the same before and after it is reflected.

lens: a transparent object with at least one spherical (curved) surface. A convex lens is fatter in the middle than at its edges. Light rays passing through such a lens are refracted and converge (come together). Concave lenses are thinner in the middle than at their edges. Light rays passing through a concave lens are refracted so that they diverge (spread apart).

magenta: a pinkish color made by adding blue and red light or subtracting green light from white light.

magnification: the ratio of the image size to the actual size of the object.

myopia: nearsightedness. People with myopia frequently have eyeballs that are longer than normal. Diverging rays of light from near objects can be focused on the retina, but the nearly parallel rays from distant objects are refracted too much and converge in front of the retina.

nucleus: the tiny central core of an atom, which contains positively charged protons along with neutrons, which carry no charge but have the same mass as the protons.

plane mirror: a mirror with a perfectly flat reflecting surface.

prism: a transparent solid with triangular bases and rectangular sides. It is often used to produce a spectrum of refracted light.

real image: an image that can be seen on a screen. Such images are produced when light is reflected from a concave mirror, refracted by a convex lens, or sent through a pinhole.

reflection: the bouncing of light off an object.

refraction: the bending of light as it passes from one transparent material to another.

rod cells: cells in the retina of the eye. They are most abundant outside the central part of the retina (fovea) and respond to dim light but not to color.

total internal reflection: all light striking the surface of a transparent substance at an angle equal to or greater than the critical angle is reflected within the substance; no refracted light emerges.

virtual image: an image that cannot be seen on a screen, such as the image seen in a plane mirror. It consists of diverging reflected or refracted light rays that appear to come from the points where the image is seen.

yellow: the color found when red and green light are added together or when blue light is subtracted from white light.

UNITS AND THEIR ABBREVIATIONS

LENGTH

English	*Metric*
mile (mi)	kilometer (km)
yard (yd)	meter (m)
foot (ft)	centimeter (cm)
inch (in.)	millimeter (mm)

AREA

English	*Metric*
square mile (mi^2)	square kilometer (km^2)
square yard (yd^2)	square meter (m^2)
square foot (ft^2)	square centimeter (cm^2)
square inch ($in.^2$)	square millimeter (mm^2)

VOLUME

English	*Metric*
cubic mile (mi^3)	cubic kilometer (km^3)
cubic yard (yd^3)	cubic meter (m^3)
cubic foot (ft^3)	cubic centimeter (cm^3)
cubic inch ($in.^3$)	cubic millimeter (mm^3)
ounce (oz)	liter (L)
	milliliter (mL)

MASS

English	*Metric*
pound (lb)	kilogram (kg)
ounce (oz)	gram (g)

TIME

hour (hr)
minute (min)
second (s)

FORCE OR WEIGHT

English
ounce (oz)
pound (lb)

Metric
newton (N)

SPEED OR VELOCITY

English
miles per hour (mi/hr)
miles per second (mi/s)
feet per second (ft/s)

Metric
kilometers per hour (km/hr)
kilometers per second (km/s)
meters per second (m/s)
centimeters per second (cm/s)

TEMPERATURE

English
degrees Fahrenheit (°F)

Metric
degrees Celsius (°C)

ENERGY

calorie (cal)
Calorie (Cal)
joule (J)

POWER

watt (W) = joule per second (J/s)

ELECTRICAL UNITS

volt (V)
ampere (A)

MATERIALS

35-mm slide
45-45-90 prism
black plastic tape
blocks
boards
bright flashlight
cardboard
cardboard box
cardboard or metal tubes, such as mailing tubes
chalkboard erasers
clay
clear piece of plastic
clear plastic tumblers
colored sheets of cellophane, plastic, or gels used in theaters (red,
    green, blue, cyan, magenta, yellow)
compact disc
convex lenses, various focal lengths
dark paper
food coloring
glue
hammer
heavy book
hypo (obtain from a photography store)
key
lamps (study lamps with cone-shaped metal shades)
large clear jar with screw-on lid

light bulbs (white, frosted, blue, green, and red)
low-power helium-neon laser
marking pen
meter stick or yardstick
microscope slide
mirrors
nail
newspapers
optical fiber light guide or optical fibers (available at a hobby store
  or a scientific supply house)
paper
pencils
phonograph record
protractor
rough surface (flattened egg carton)
ruler
scissors
shoebox
sink
slide projector
spring-type clothespins
studio proof paper (available at a photography store)
T-pin
tape
tray
waxed paper
white stick
white cards

INDEX

ABOUT THE AUTHOR

Robert Gardner, science educator and award-winning author of nonfiction for young people, has written over fifty books to introduce readers to the wonders of science. A *School Library Journal* reviewer has called him "the master of the science experiment book."

He earned a B.A. from Wesleyan University and an M.A. from Trinity College. Before retiring, he taught biology, chemistry, physics, and physical science for over thirty years at Salisbury School in Salisbury, Connecticut. He and his wife, Natalie, reside in Massachusetts where he serves as a consultant on science education and continues to write books for future scientists.